EVERY LAST THING

Also by Alyse Knorr:

Wolf Tours
Ardor
Mega-City Redux
Copper Mother
Annotated Glass

Every Last Thing

Alyse Knorr

THE WORD WORKS
WASHINGTON D.C.

Every Last Thing © 2025 Alyse Knorr

Reproduction of any part of this book
in any form or by any means, electronic or mechanical,
except when quoted in part for the purpose of review,
must be with permission in writing
from the publisher.

Address inquiries to:
THE WORD WORKS
P.O. Box 42164
Washington, D.C. 20015
editor@wordworksbooks.org
No part of this book may be used
or reproduced in any manner
for the purpose of training
artificial intelligence
technologies
or systems.
Ever.

Cover art: Diana Schmertz
Cover design: Susan Pearce
Interior Design: Emma Berver
Author photograph: Regis University

LCCN: 2023944857
ISBN: 978-1-944585-77-8

Acknowledgments

Many thanks to the editors of the following journals, where these poems first appeared:

BOAT Press: "Perhaps"
The Cincinnati Review: "Artifacts [I wrote you a letter]"
Dream Pop Journal: "Note Pressed into Your Palm"
DREGINALD: "Offering," "Conversation," and "Working"
The Figure 1: "Why Is the Measure of Love Loss"
Gigantic Sequins: "Log"
Hobart: "Queer Apparitional," "Scare Tactics," "The Scariest Thing," and "Unknown Knowns"
Interim: "The Paradox of Self-Reference," "Activity Report," "The Lyric Address," and "A Pearl on Your Finger"
Leveler: "15th & G"
Metatron: "Known Knowns," "Known Unknowns," and "Unknown Unknowns"
NightBlock: "Scattered Forecast" and "Units"
Nimrod: "List" and "Measurements"
Press Pause Press: "The Desire of the Moth for the Star," "Less Than Everything Cannot Satisfy Man," "Trouble," and "Evening"
Sorority Mansion Year of the Dog: "The Abstract" and "Self-Assessment"
Spoon River Poetry Review: "It's Been a Big Week"
Touch the Donkey: "Gratification"
Whiskey Island: "Day I Wanted Only One Thing"
Wildness: "Epistle"
Word For/Word: "Hose Me Down," "O Breath," "O O," "O Reserve"

Contents

I

Scattered Forecast	5
Conversation	6
Artifacts	7
Emptied Full	8
Queer Apparitional	9
Working	10
Today	11
In the Summer	12
Day I Wanted Every Last Thing	13
Day I Wanted Only One Thing	14
Evening	15
O Breath	16
O Reserve	17
O O	18
Offering	19
Trouble	20
Log	21
The Desire of the Moth for the Star	22
The Paradox of Self-Reference	23

II

15th & G	27
Self-Assessment	28
Measurements	29
The Abstract	30
Scare Tactics	31
The Scariest Thing	32
Less Than Everything Cannot Satisfy Man	33
A Pearl on Your Finger	34
Sensory Detail	35

Known Knowns	36
Known Unknowns	37
Unknown Knowns	38
Unknown Unknowns	39
List	40
Artifacts	41
Units	42

III

Why Is the Measure of Love Loss	45
Gratification	46
Potentiality	47
Hose Me Down	48
It's Been a Big Week	49
Origins	50
The Lyric Address	51
Reciprocity	52
Perhaps	53
Interview	54
Activity Report	55
Manifest	56
[Apology]	57
Note Pressed into Your Palm	58
Tag	59
Swamp Preserve	60
Epistle (*you*)	61

Notes	63
About the Author / About the Artist	65
About The Word Works	66
Other Word Works Books	67

] heart
] absolutely
] I can
]

—Sappho, trans. Anne Carson

I

Scattered Forecast

first thing in the morning my mouth all full
of dirt—you're at the bottom of the pool
having a tea party   you're riding the subway
reading a book   you're a few years early
I'm a few years late   you're a bus ride away
& one different turn   a sentimental letter
a dissection of words   you're the only chair
in the room   you're pulling down a mountain
you're running through the zoo   you're winding
up your alarm clock   you're drinking beer from
a boot   you're so loud I'm amazed I heard you
you're so quiet I'm amazed I did not   you're a row
of tiny pictures   mirror to the sky   you're
refracting the light in your many-prismed heart while
I dance around too late in my time capsule of rain

Conversation

all day my blood stays in my body   remarkable   or
as the pope might say   *ad majorem dei gloriam*   my body
a tower in itself   a list of other sins   for the copy machine
65 Glorias   for each forgotten name   80 apostles 80
creeds   above the boiled river   two drones for hands
or one sad elevator   in this bed   an emergency   Gabriel
in the dream   plastic & immaculate   for other sins
I dip my fist to river beds   pray to Mary & to Mary's son
for the hands   pray to pops   begotten   again   they say
tickling their hearts   *what eyes turn thou upward*   beseeching
a litany of error   in their X-ray gowns   a great sum:
what is authentic   they ask   & I flagellate an answer

Artifacts

I wrote you the letter so you could tell
me how it's wrong   the iron gate
you never saw   the plate I washed
that set you off   my grandfather—
not grandmother—dead of a stroke
in the kitchen   moving my books
from room to room   my bed in
and out of the closet   you stop to calm
your dog every several paces   and
he does   I wrote you the rubric
and you changed one thing   halfway
through the book   halfway through
the halfway chapter   weeping on
my unborn daughter's floor   coconut
scrubbed raw in my hair   a caribou
named Star   my daughter named almost
the same as you   the world felt larger
then   you said the word *world*   bereft

Emptied Full

too much much
today   my over-

stimulated   eyes
rapidly sleep   it off

in the doubled bed
in the diorama

behind the museum
a bird saying potpourri

another saying hey no
hey no   trucks

everywhere   & planes
an extra E in week

the robot dog   who
can let himself out

& your stupid trochaic
name   on my arm

still I am stilled by this
bombardment   this

free supply   this total
storm of items

Queer Apparitional

let's say we say nothing
ever happened
wipe our brains

clean then press
play from
the beginning—

if new   say new:
when will you get
here   & where
will we meet

& what can I not
invent from this
terrible long night

Working

at the condensery
looking for you

out the foggy
window   I ate

a whole bar
of soap   I wore

my very best shirt
if only you could see

if only your voice
could directly enter

my ear drums
& beat beat beat

them into some
common kind of sense

Today

the sun was so goddamn bright
the snow on the mountains was there

a man on the street saluted me
& I never asked why

the trees stood up on the ground
like perfectly capable beings

how dare they do such a thing
how dare they move their branches

like that   touching the air
like hands across a face

In the Summer

I climb up my in-
sides, all 10 mg
& a moon secret,
mouth talking back
into itself—no
more I said & you
said only a little /
thank God I got
my saw back first
thank God the rat
turned into a cat
toy the week the
crow died at my
feet—I can only
contain so much
after all   this all

Day I Wanted Every Last Thing

to compress   to contain it all
in one imagined moment—
like a marble world spilled from a
cup or how I can hear out
my window the birds & you
humming a soft song that
if I could write this down
would explain it all at once

Day I Wanted Only One Thing

I did not want an apple
did not want lunch   I was
too expansive for any
planet   my limbs cramped
& aching   not around you
my lungs cooped up   encaged
& of course my awful hands
I was so sick of language
the letters the words an alphabet
of pointless sounds   give me
brand new eyes I told the sun
you could give me those
at the very least

Evening

in your blue dress at the top
of the slide: your shoulders

& your knees & all those
nights I stared at the wall steel

limbed while the Top 40 played
occasionally your elbow

touched my arm & I bobbed
along not waving but drowning

did I shoot some gull from
the sky   did I kiss the poison

mouth of some talented witch
did I dare to eat a peach

what is the story behind this
shore I'm all washed up upon

O Breath

Say two girls in a room
each drink their own tea
one feels a scalpel-bear
tapping in her chest
one asks the other:
what color is your heart
one's horoscope reads:
loves the wanting

O Reserve

Again today I
   plastic diorama
at all costs avoid
   the eyes or melt
on contact astray
   ashore this terrible
new stirring   at
   great cost I have
gazed directly upon
   the surface—I
file this wire to
   say nothing direct
& nothing
   barely even true

O O

But they keep my heart
online   my bones a system
of pulleys & gears   in this
whole mall   the only girl
set to fucking explode   dogs
running around   in my
synapsed brain that eats
all the sparks itself—
O here is a tree & here
another   both staggeringly
tragically sad
                I used to
be the tree but now I am
the branches—no
now I am the gaps

Offering

are you as scared of
you as I am & how
   do you measure it?
once I drew you a
mountain & you knew
   exactly what it meant

Trouble

you came from cold   stuttering
wrenched engine   & red ribbon
cream   oh   pitch your tent
dear   I'm quaking   taut & pure
envisioned   lying on your side
& me   a pile of elbows   more
stable   nailed down   in this great
shortage of houses   near extinct
& virused   the feature begins
heel chained   new kind of debt
oh darling   let's make for
the woods   no   love   sit there
& speak   forever on   nothing
I'm all tuned in

Log

even on the goddamn
glacier / even in the sun
/ immediate morning &
lingering night / when
I take a bite of my turkey
& garlic sandwich / when
I apologize to my poor
hands / two dogs eager
& dumb & ever so tamed

The Desire of the Moth for the Star

is this that story again with the wings
& the sun   once you told me about your
limitless want   you told me   you told
me   yet still I'm all burning up   can you
read the smoky letters   can you smell
the charred-down wood   once you told
me about a girl with wings   & it was me

The Paradox of Self-Reference

so full of wanting   I forget my name again
        pile crushed down to a swirl of sounds:
        the sounds of indecision, of sex, of glee,
& at the end a lisped arrival to the place I never left—
        cat's scratch cornea and the smell of coconut
        forever   a model of loss tucked in with all
the smeared maps of having   mark my words
        I did find myself   sketched on the wall
        of that basement   I knew my place
as a dot in the code   a whole city of desire   knew that
        if I contain everything I cannot include myself
        tame me, retain me I sang *hold me faster while I sink*

II

15th & G

tried to lose my mind but the grid stayed
the same / maybe a car hit me / maybe
I was struck / dumb /maybe my hair blew
in the alley wind the way you'd like / all
swept up in the fucking now / O I ran
like a deer & you took one good look &
soft jogged away / I yelled & you took
my yell / you took my hands / you left
the numb outline of your print / you
don't have eyes / you never did /
you were a voice / you were a sound /
an empty imagined train / can you see
this mountain with your mouth / can
you let me know it's there / & my
mind rusting over back to normal /
what does that sound like / tell me / tell
me in numbers / tell me in notes

Self-Assessment

saw a pretty girl & I cut off my arms
I was so full of day I could die   my
body slow eating itself in that public
place   in that public place   it was just
like PacMan   the guilt eating the fear
the love eating the guilt the only person
I wanted to tell was you   the only
person who could make something
of it was you   I wanted to hand you
every last thing   I wanted your head
in my lap   I wanted to make you a gift
of this whole papered over planet

Measurements

you said practice was the plan but
practice was the problem: you led
me like a horse by the mouth   you
touched your ribs & felt mine   you
bit your fingers & bit mine   there
is a place behind the ear   a movement
of the tendons   in your forearm
a certain number of bones   in every
spine a certain magnitude of *yes*

The Abstract

meds making my muscles twitch
is one way to begin   one way
of three   no more   but less:
a concept you've always been
concerned with   I have never been
a rash entity   but I have grown
concerned with hurling the orange
bottle into the boreal snowy
woods to see if a genie would
smoke out   recite my heart rate
to me   in metronomic beats
per minute   my thoughts
a harpooned animal   a bullet
train   & every other sorry
thing   does this discussion
concern you   are you concerned
are you getting high off my art
am i as good in the abstract as
in the wet city grass at night

Scare Tactics

I grew hands by the dozen
I was a generalized reaching
clasping monster   it was
not a dream shared or
otherwise   it was neither
yours nor mine nor ours

The Scariest Thing

today I'm a tough guy—
digging up holes & eating
all the dirt   when I'm not
clear I was never clear
when I am I was never not
today I toughly learned
that four screams means
SOS   then you said words
mean little when they
come from your mouth
it hit me like a riddle
like a riddle or a joke

Less Than Everything Cannot Satisfy Man

an evil thing this reaching
this kudzu choked low
round the waist   it grows
to live   it kills to grow
it ends not ever   beautiful
things are made of fire
& fire burns

A Pearl on Your Finger

sealed   sea led down
to sand   a hook pierced
through my lonesome
hand   I refuse this body
its singularity   I refuse
the collapse of time
the unity of a moment
that can only be one

Sensory Detail

I can hear all the way to Atlanta!
the ring wrapped newly round
your finger! the ring of that ring
tremendous & profound like
that time you were inches from
my face at your play! so much
motion I could barely find you
in the chorus   but when I saw
you see me & recognize   & when
I saw you forget your next line—

Known Knowns

sounds I care not
to specify   the
information age
of 32 when know-
ledge & power
part & disperse
like two moths
untangled into ones

Known Unknowns

the sound of water
near your childhood
home   your first
anything   your first
everything   the way
you learned to speak
the words they taught
you   where they began
& where they ended

Unknown Knowns

listen: I've learned a brand new way
of seeing   through hard & soft eyes
I've learned I may be a fixed
& limited animal   I may know
what is happening   but not how
we may be entangled by spooky
actions   and maybe I only awakened
just when I thought I had slept

Unknown Unknowns

most dangerous of all—
none know   none unknow-
able   to unknow   to stay
in my corner of the tipped
world & know the ice:
how cold how known
secure even in its melting

List

less the way I looked:
the way I made things
an alchemy   a power
just behind the lips
how art can sweep
you up   make you
riot the theater   hurt
whoever's closest
that dissonance   that
infection   dug into
the lines   but
you left me at the
subway   you left me
at the gate   I could see
it in small hungry words
before I ever saw it at all

Artifacts

green tea late at night   cigars as stars or a porch light   I washed your dishes   sat outside your door the concrete table   terrier that drew too close   laid out my hands   palms facing Saturn   an unwalkable surface   made whole   from a pulling force   you hated how late it could get   but you always wore a watch   you drew me rugby plays on a napkin the gymnasts on-screen holding each other up   and me quaking in the frame   prairie grass bending underfoot   slippery you   already gone and never coming back

Units

minutes photos
pounds per day

boils down to
what you wanted

my very bones
 here I am

a narrow skeleton
on a narrow street

in a sunless city
in a snowy bowl

III

Why Is the Measure of Love Loss

in the midst of the sceneless day
we enter the burning building

of course this is a dream   yet
when I looked over the stern for

an answer—when I closed
my eyes & sent you a picture

you saw a girl dancing ballet
& "behold! the pinnacle was

dismantled; the glory of
the vintage was dust" &

wonder ceased entirely to be
wonder   next was the part

with the wolfthicket—with
the wolf baring her great neck

what I mean to say is: ten years
ago I stood in the street

with you   now each day I eat
a pill the size of a doll's eye—

my sleep quiet as a clean white room
my teeth all chewed up to chalk

Gratification

cranes hang my hands
from the skyline   & a
mountain eats my name

I was all in the minute
they pulled back the curtain
for the sake of science

& a free meal   then the
aftershocks far worse
& the problem of one-way time

if I didn't know on the glacier
then I never really knew—
forever holes   he called them

because you fall through the ice
forever & forever never stops

Potentiality

Now that the now is back
you can trip and sink,
see the green demon

with your CV and bio
standing at the lectern
clicking through slides—

you live in a face and
a jacket, think once per day
of an unspeakable day, and

it's too soon to search for
methods yet here they are
beneath prevention.

You know now in the now
the accident of love—not
a joyful theory but an ember,

not a dreamline but a plot.
And shouldn't you be plotted?
Last you checked, the creature

was half out of the piano
reaching for you—for the
very throat you use to sing.

Hose Me Down

were they
ever notified
my backbone
lips finger-
tips did the
forward time
devour imagined
or is your head
still in my lap
like a pretty
auburn ghost

It's Been a Big Week

suture my phone directly
to my chest   *here*   heart-
spotting the spot   you could
see in the cold air   if you
had been there with me
like you were—no   a
cauterization   hot & elect-
ric   a tickle   a bolt   a great
sweeping   that could mean
the start or end of pulse

Origins

what if I'd been sleeping till
just last week wrapped in the
flag of my home planet & its
rings   what would such a
story look like   & would I
then be as gallant as I aspire?

The Lyric Address

illusion of privacy
space behind water
back of the fall
you liked my lists—
I never heard yours

let's try to meet
you said   try to
touch   push the limits
of this sacred dull order
why not leap off this

thought into ten million
more   why not see
what it's like   newness
for the sake of the new

Reciprocity

was it a boundary or
a scale   what tool
can best measure
the input & lack
O crack me open &
curtain the window
I dare you   I'll glow

Perhaps

that black hole was meant to form
out on the street in front of my
house   in your car   a possum
chasing a cat across the road   a
helicopter slicing up the air   & no
room to twist away   perhaps
acting is a genetic talent   perhaps
learned   if dreams require discipline
we had best get started   take me to
your outside room   hoist me over
the wrought iron fence   show me the
pretty graves   the way the moon
sounds shadowed on the lawn

Interview

was it the newness
or the old soul way

what stock should I
place into which account

O I cannot ask even
one thing of you—

you who saw into my
X-ray heart & called it

heads   tails   yes
no   how could you

be so careless   how
did this occur

why not leave me
in the brilliant dark

where I was gone &
done but warm?

Activity Report

tie a bell around my neck
so you'll hear me coming
I'm warning you   O how
I am   coming   noise full
can't help what came   or
what's to come   here in
the hot coming nights come
on   I know   how you worry
I know   how that sounds
but for just one night
it was exactly like a song

Manifest

O my noisy heart
O my bombed-out
soul   yes I said it
stupid trees   stupid
mountains   I will be
as artless as I like
sincerity is my means
my end over end   over-
wrought   test   whether
I can cram it all back to
my bottom stomach parts
feel it raw my throat
the whole way down

[Apology]

do not say what you'll
say   do not tell them
what you've told them
wrap it up like a present
tap it out in a mean code
bury it in a trash pit
for thousands of years
& when it's found
it won't be too mean
to mean   it won't be
too late   as long
as it isn't too loud

Note Pressed into Your Palm

if a body
takes shape

when spoken
spoken to

spoken of
spoken for

then why
name it why

not leave
why not

never think
on it at all

Tag

take care
take it in
to your
sternum
know its
thrum pitch
yaw barbaric
feel it under
the soft vest
of your skin

Swamp Preserve

if every new thought has been thought already
if distance is measured in rain and it rains here
every day   if the man cuts down the ghost iris
because scarcity yields value   if only a year ago
you didn't know my name   if sweat dampens
the hair trailing down your neck   if it rains again
today and starts another fire   if the strangler fig
tightens around the waist of the cypress   then
when will this world end so the new one can begin?

Epistle

(you)

in the blue dark trees
with their wet heat
& their terrible branches
in a room with a window
& a bed   in a room with
a small table for writing
on the backs of envelopes
in Brazil   where you've never
been   in the bottoms of my
waking dreams   in the
middle of the street shouting
like God   in my whole
limitless life   in the morning
in the big noisy city   in
a cathedral made of cream
marble & stone   in a rivered
glass of wine   in a wedding
dress   inside this thought as
it shakes itself clean   in the
park with the statue of Yeats
& the leaves eating the sun
we sat under   in every single
day   in an hour   in the
children   in the sea   in an
envelope I forgot I mailed
myself a long long time ago

Notes

In "Conversation," the phrase "a tower in itself" is borrowed from mathematician Dr. Bethany Springer.

In "Self-Assessment," the phrase "in that public place in that public place" is borrowed from Olga Broumas's "Amazon Twins."

"Queer Apparitional" takes its title from Terry Castle's book *The Apparitional Lesbian*.

"Working" is after Lorine Niedecker's "Poet's Work."

In "Evening," the phrase "not waving but drowning" is borrowed from the title of a poem by Stevie Smith. This poem also engages with Samuel Taylor Coleridge's "The Rime of the Ancient Mariner."

"The Desire of the Moth for the Star" takes its title from a line in Percy Bysshe Shelley's "To —."

"Less Than Everything Cannot Satisfy Man" takes its title from a quote by William Blake.

"Why is the Measure of Love Loss" takes its title from the first line in Jeanette Winterson's book *Written on the Body*. The quoted phrase in this poem is borrowed from Thomas De Quincey's "Dream Fugue."

Many of these poems appeared in an artist's book called *Why Is the Measure of Love Loss*, a collaboration with artist Diana Schmertz. For more on this project, and on Diana's work, please visit dianaschmertz.com/collaboration.

My deep gratitude to all at The Word Works for giving this manuscript such a wonderful home, and to Nancy White and Emma Berver for their excellent design and editorial work.

Thank you to Regis University's Faculty Development Committee for the grant funding that helped make this book possible, and to Homestead National Monument for providing invaluable time and space on the prairie to write it. I am deeply grateful to all of my students and colleagues at Regis, and in particular my current and former English Department colleagues Eric Baus, Mark Bruhn, J'Lyn Chapman, Scott Dimovitz, David Hicks, Frank McGill, Lara Narcisi, Daryl Palmer, and Andrea Rexilius. For their generous feedback on these poems, thank you to Sammie Downing, Siwar Masannat, Violet Mitchell, Kate Partridge, Darby Price, and Diana Schmertz. Thank you to Lucy Knorr-Partridge and Calvin Knorr-Partridge for the joyful gift of their existence.

This book, as always, is for Kate.

About the Author

Alyse Knorr is an associate professor of English at Regis University and co-editor of Switchback Books. She is the author of the poetry collections *Wolf Tours* (2024); *Ardor* (2023), a Lambda Literary Award finalist; *Mega-City Redux* (2017); *Copper Mother* (2016); and *Annotated Glass* (2013). She also authored the video game history books *GoldenEye* (2022) and *Super Mario Bros. 3* (2016) and four poetry chapbooks. Her work has appeared in *The New Republic*, POETRY *Magazine*, *Alaska Quarterly Review*, *Denver Quarterly*, and *The Georgia Review*, among others. She received her MFA from George Mason University.

About the Artist

Diana Schmertz started her art career in Amsterdam, Holland as a recipient of De Ateliers 63' grant and residency program. Schmertz has received many grants and awards from organizations such as the Lower Manhattan Cultural Council, the Northern Manhattan Arts Alliance, the Aljira Emerge Fellowship program, and the Drawing Center. She has participated in residencies in Russia, Europe and the U.S.. Some solo shows include: They Are Each Other For A While, at Zillman Museum of Art, Bangor Maine, Soma, Muriel Guépin Gallery LES, NYC, "Don't Say Other", Art House Gallery, Jersey City, NJ, and Systemic Constructs for the Reduction of Uncertainty, at Garis & Hahn, in conjunction with Ideas City Biennial Festival sponsored by the New Museum, NYC. Schmertz has made public art supported by multiple grants. Some include Declarations on Human Rights, presented through CHaShaMa & New York City Department of Transportation at Fordham Plaza, Bronx, NY and a permanent work at 125th Street Carnegie Library commissioned by the NYC Department of Cultural Affairs Percent for Art Program in collaboration with New York Public Library and the Economic Development Corporation

About The Word Works

Since its founding in 1974, The Word Works has steadily published volumes of contemporary poetry and presented public programs. Its imprints include The Washington Prize, The Tenth Gate Prize, The Hilary Tham Capital Collection, and International Editions.

Monthly, The Word Works offers free programs in its Café Muse Literary Salon. Starting in 2023, the winners of the Jacklyn Potter Young Poets Competition will be presented in the June Café Muse program.

As a 501(c)3 organization, The Word Works has received awards from the National Endowment for the Arts, the National Endowment for the Humanities, the D.C. Commission on the Arts & Humanities, the Witter Bynner Foundation, Poets & Writers, The Writer's Center, Bell Atlantic, the David G. Taft Foundation, and others, including many generous private patrons.

An archive of artistic and administrative materials in the Washington Writing Archive is housed in the George Washington University Gelman Library. The Word Works is a member of the Community of Literary Magazines and Presses.

wordworksbooks.org

Other Word Works Books

Annik Adey-Babinski, *Okay Cool No Smoking Love Pony*
Karren L. Alenier, *From the Belly: Poets Respond to Gertrude Stein's Tender Buttons*
Karren L. Alenier, *Wandering on the Outside*
Emily August, *The Punishments Must Be a School*
Jennifer Barber, *The Sliding Boat Our Bodies Made*
Andrea Carter Brown, *September 12*
Willa Carroll, *Nerve Chorus*
Grace Cavalieri, *Creature Comforts / The Long Game: Poems Selected & New*
Abby Chew, *A Bear Approaches from the Sky*
Nadia Colburn, *The High Shelf*
Henry Crawford, *The Binary Planet*
Barbara Goldberg, *Berta Broadfoot and Pepin the Short / Breaking & Entering: New and Selected Poems*
Akua Lezli Hope, *Them Gone*
Michael Klein, *The Early Minutes of Without: Poems Selected & New*
Deborah Kuan, *Women on the Moon*
Frannie Lindsay, *If Mercy*
Elaine Magarrell, *The Madness of Chefs*
Chloe Martinez, *Ten Thousand Selves*
Marilyn McCabe, *Glass Factory*
JoAnne McFarland, *Identifying the Body*
Leslie McGrath, *Feminists Are Passing from Our Lives*
Kevin McLellan, *Ornitheology*
Ron Mohring, *The Boy Who Reads in the Trees*
A. Molotkov, *Future Symptoms*
Ann Pelletier, *Letter That Never*
W.T. Pfefferle, *My Coolest Shirt*
Ayaz Pirani, *Happy You Are Here*
Robert Sargent, *Aspects of a Southern Story / A Woman from Memphis*
Roger Smith, *Radiation Machine Gun Funk*
Jeddie Sophonius, *Love & Sambal*
Julia Story, *Spinster for Hire*
Barbara Ungar, *Naming the Animals*
Cheryl Clark Vermeulen, *They Can Take It Out*
Julie Marie Wade, *Skirted*

Miles Waggener, *Superstition Freeway*
Fritz Ward, *Tsunami Diorama*
Camille-Yvette Welsch, *The Four Ugliest Children in Christendom*
Amber West, *Hen & God*
Maceo Whitaker, *Narco Farm*

www.ingramcontent.com/pod-product-compliance
Lightning Source LLC
Chambersburg PA
CBHW050034090426
42735CB00022B/3485